The Natural World
AUSTRALIA

Jenna Myers

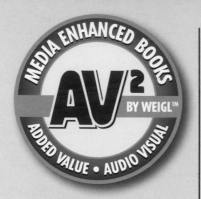

AV² provides enriched content that supplements and complements this book. Weigl's AV² books strive to create inspired learning and engage young minds in a total learning experience.

Your AV² Media Enhanced books come alive with...

Audio
Listen to sections of the book read aloud.

Key Words
Study vocabulary, and complete a matching word activity.

Go to www.av2books.com, and enter this book's unique code.

Video
Watch informative video clips.

Quizzes
Test your knowledge.

BOOK CODE

D 262227

Embedded Weblinks
Gain additional information for research.

Slide Show
View images and captions, and prepare a presentation.

AV² by Weigl brings you media enhanced books that support active learning.

Try This!
Complete activities and hands-on experiments.

... and much, much more!

Published by AV² by Weigl
350 5th Avenue, 59th Floor
New York, NY 10118
Websites: www.av2books.com   www.weigl.com

Library of Congress Cataloging-in-Publication Data

Myers, Jenna, author.
 Australia / Jenna Myers.
    pages cm. -- (The natural world)
 Includes index.
 ISBN 978-1-4896-0946-5 (hardcover : alk. paper) -- ISBN 978-1-4896-0947-2 (softcover : alk. paper) -- ISBN 978-1-4896-0948-9 (single user ebk.)
-- ISBN 978-1-4896-0949-6 (multi user ebk.)
1. Natural history--Australia--Juvenile literature. 2. Ecology--Australia--Juvenile literature.
3. Australia--Environmental conditions--Juvenile literature. I. Title.
 QH197.M94 2015
 578.0994--dc23
                              2014004672

Printed in the United States of America in North Mankato, Minnesota
1 2 3 4 5 6 7 8 9 0 18 17 16 15 14

042014
WEP150314

Editor: Heather Kissock
Design: Mandy Christiansen

Every reasonable effort has been made to trace ownership and to obtain permission to reprint copyright material. The publishers would be pleased to have any errors or omissions brought to their attention so that they may be corrected in subsequent printings.

Weigl acknowledges Getty Images as its primary image supplier for this title.
Page 17L: Marion Anstis.

Contents

Welcome to Australia!

Australia is the only country on Earth that is also a continent. It is one of the largest countries in the world, covering 2,969,907 square miles (7,692,024 square kilometers). It is also the driest inhabited continent in the world. Australia's landscape is varied. It includes desert areas, hills, mountains, and tropical **rainforests**. Its coastal areas have long beaches and **coral reefs**. Australia's largest deserts are in an area known as the Outback. Little water or vegetation is found in the Outback, and the temperatures are very high.

The diversity in landscapes has created environments for a wide variety of plants and animals. Australia is home to about 27,700 plant **species**. It also has about 378 mammal, 828 bird, and 4,000 fish species. A variety of amphibians and marine mammals live there as well. Many of Earth's deadliest animals, including funnel-web spiders and venomous snakes, are found on the continent as well. This **biodiversity** makes Australia an interesting place to explore.

Australia has about 10% of the world's biodiversity.

Australia has more than 140 species of marsupials. This animal group includes kangaroos, wallabies, koalas, and wombats.

Kangaroos and wallabies vary in size and weight, ranging from 2.2 to 198.4 pounds (1 to 90 kilograms).

Kangaroos are endemic to Australia and are the only large animals that hop to move about.

Unique Australian Life

Australia is unusual for its endemic species. Endemic species are plants and animals that are found only in a particular place or region. One reason people visit Australia is to see plants and animals that cannot be found anywhere else in the world. More than 80 percent of Australia's plants, mammals, reptiles, and frogs are endemic. Some of Australia's best-known endemic animals are the kangaroo, the koala, the platypus, the echidna, and the wombat.

Koalas spend most of their time in trees. Their sharp claws help them maintain a tight grip on the branches.

Tasmania is an island found off the southern coast of Australia. The island was once attached to Australia, but became separated from the mainland millions of years ago. Over time, Tasmania's land and climate changed. Many unique plants and animals began to develop on the island as a result. These species occur naturally in Tasmania and nowhere else. The Tasmanian native hen, the yellow wattlebird, and the black-headed honeyeater are just a few examples of the endemic bird species found here. The Huon pines are the island's oldest living trees and an example of one of Tasmania's most famous endemic plants. Although Tasmania belongs to Australia, it is a separate place with its own rare biodiversity.

Tasmania

Australia

Tasmania ──●

Up to 70% of Tasmania's alpine plants are endemic.

The Tasmanian devil has one of the strongest bites of any land mammal.

Tasmania has 12 species of endemic birds.

Scientists believe that about 300 Tasmanian tigers live on the island.

The call of a Tasmanian tree frog sounds like a duck.

A Huon pine can live to be 3,000 years old.

Where in the World?

Australia lies between the Pacific, Indian, and Southern Oceans, in the Southern Hemisphere. It is approximately 2,500 miles (4,000 km) from east to west and 2,000 miles (3,200 km) from north to south. Its coastline is more than 22,800 miles (36,735 km) long. Due to the size of the continent, the climate varies drastically from place to place. Australia is a land of extreme temperatures. These temperatures can range from highs of 104°F (40°C) in parts of the central desert to below freezing in the higher regions of the southeast. Northern Australia usually has warm weather year round. Southern regions experience seasonal changes, with cooler winters. Rainfall in Australia varies over most of the continent. Average rainfall is less than 23 inches (600 millimeters).

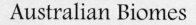

ASIA

INDIAN OCEAN

AUSTRALIA

SOUTH PACIFIC OCEAN

ARTICA

Australian Biomes

Biomes are areas with the similar climate, terrain, plants, and animals. There are similar biomes all over the world. However, the types of plants and animals found in each biome can be distinct between continents. Australia has several land biomes. These include chaparral, grassland, desert, and forest.

The dry climate makes forest fires in the mountains of Australia a constant threat during lightning storms.

Map of Australian Biomes

ASIA

INDIAN
OCEAN

AUSTRALIA

SOUTHERN
OCEAN

Legend

Chaparral

Desert   Rainforest

Grassland   Fresh water

Mixed Forest   Ocean

0   500 Miles

0   500 Kilometers

Australian Land Biomes

Each type of biome has a different set of characteristics. Australia's biomes all have similar characteristics to the corresponding biomes on other continents. The types of animals and plants that live in the biomes also share similar traits. However, there will be distinctions between these organisms depending on where they live in each biome.

Desert

Although Australia has plenty of fertile land, more than one-third of it is covered in desert. Many different kinds of plants and animals can be found within Australia's 10 major deserts.

Plants: There are approximately 1,800 types of plants found in Australian deserts. The most common type of vegetation is a class of grasses called spinifex. Other plant life includes acacias and small shrubs. The desert is home to a large number of rare plant species as well.

Animals: There are more than 605 **vertebrates** found in Australia's deserts. Desert mammals include the red kangaroo, the bilby, and the dingo. Insects such as grasshoppers, crickets, beetles, and grubs dominate the desert environment.

Winter
−4 °to 68°F
(−20° to 20°C)
Summer
77° to 120°F
(25° to 49°C)

Rainfall
Less than
20" (51 cm)
per year

Australia is isolated from other continents, which explains its varied temperatures, rainfall, and plant and animal life. Although Australia has deserts and rainforests like other parts of the world, much of the vegetation and wildlife within its rainforests is different. This is because of Australia's location and isolation compared to the other continents.

Rainforest

Australia has both tropical and temperate rainforests. Tropical rainforests are found in warm climates close to the **equator**. Temperate rainforests grow in the cooler climate of the southeast and throughout Tasmania.

Plants: Many native fruit trees, including figs and green plums, are found in the tropical regions. Primitive plants live in Australia's rainforests. They are similar to those growing more than 100 million years ago.

Animals: Rainforest animals include koalas, opossums, platypuses, flying foxes, and lyrebirds.

Annual Temperature 68° to 93°F (20° to 34°C)

Rainfall 47 to 118" (120 to 300 cm) per year

Grassland

Grassland is a flat, open plain that is mainly covered in grass. Grassland areas support varieties of other plants, including wildflowers, trees, and low shrubs. Grasslands in Australia are often referred to as savannas.

Plants: Along with grasses and grass-like plants, wildflowers also grow in grasslands.

Animals: Insects, birds, frogs, and reptiles can be found in grassland **habitats**. Kangaroos also live on grassland.

Summer/Winter Temperatures 37° to 100°F (3° to 38°C)

Rainfall 20 to 50" (50.8 to 127 cm) per year

Australian Ecosystems and Habitats

A biome can be made up of many different ecosystems. An ecosystem is the interaction between the living, such as plants, animals, and microbes, and the nonliving, such as air, water, and soil. An ecosystem can be large or small depending on where it is found on Earth.

Every ecosystem is made up of one or more habitats. A habitat is the place or environment where a species of plant or animal lives. That species is **adapted** to its surroundings. Habitats supply the food, water, and oxygen needed to survive. Australia's ecosystems and habitats are diverse and support a variety of unique plants and animals.

The Daintree Rainforest is known as the world's oldest tropical rainforest. It hosts a variety of habitats, including swamps, mangroves, and eucalyptus woodlands. A variety of bird species live in the Daintree, including 13 that can only be found in Australia. The Daintree is also home to one third of Australia's frog, marsupial, and reptile species.

Australia's rainforests are found in coastal areas where moisture is more plentiful.

The Flinders Ranges in South Australia are part of the desert biome. Animals in this region include the yellow-footed rock wallaby. Sturt's desert pea is one of the area's native plants.

The Nullarbor Plain covers 100,000 square miles (260,000 sq. km) of mostly flat land. The plain's vegetation is mainly saltbush and blue bush, though grasses and flowers can appear after winter rains. Rare plants and animals are strictly protected in the Nullarbor National Park.

Habitat loss is affecting the yellow-footed rock wallaby. Ten years ago, there were about 12,000 living in nature. Now, there are only about 2,000.

The Blue Mountains, in New South Wales, consist of more than 2.4 million acres (10,000 sq. km) of forests, sandstone cliffs, canyons, waterfalls, and bushland. Large eucalyptus gum trees form a thick canopy across the landscape. They emit an oily mist that mixes with dust and scatters light waves to make the mountains appear blue.

Plant Life in Australia

Australia's plant life is one of its treasures, with about 24,000 species of native plants identified. Of the estimated 20,000 species of **vascular** plants found in Australia, 16,000 are endemic to the country. Australia is home to wildflowers such as the waratah, banksia, and kangaroo paws. There are approximately 28,000 species of eucalypts and 1,000 species of acacias. Most plants and trees found in Australia, particularly in the desert areas, are tough. They can live on little water and survive scorching temperatures. Although Australia is a vast country, only about 5 percent of its land is forested.

Spinifex grasslands cover 22 percent of the Australian continent.

Spinifex

Spinifex grass can survive in the driest soils of Australia. Several species of spinifex can be spotted in the red sand desert and rocky ranges of Central Australia. The prickly dome of spinifex is home to small desert mammals and reptiles. Spinifex has very long roots that can extend up to 10 feet (3 m) into the ground to reach water.

Eucalypt Trees

Eucalypts make up almost 80 percent of Australia's forests. They are found in most parts of the continent, with the exception of high alpine areas, rainforests, and the dry interior. Native Australian animals, such as the koala, use eucalypts for shelter. Red river gums are the most widespread eucalypt. They can grow to approximately 147 feet (45 m) high and can live for hundreds of years.

Eucalypts can range in size from low shrubs to tall trees.

Acacias

The Australian acacia tree is commonly known as a "wattle." There are about 1,200 species of wattle, and 954 of these are currently recognized as growing in Australia. From coastal zones and mountains to the dry inland, wattles are a common sight. They vary from small shrubs to the tall blackwood. Acacia flowers come in all shades of yellow. Most species bloom during late winter and spring. During this time, the golden wattle blossoms with large, sweet-smelling flower heads. The golden wattle is Australia's floral emblem.

The acacia tree grows quickly but only lives for about 40 years.

Melaleuca

Melaleucas are often called "paperbarks" in the larger, tree forms and "honey myrtles" and "tea trees" in the smaller, shrub forms. This common plant species can be identified by the pale papery bark that peels from its trunk. The melaleuca ranges from the coast to the semi-arid inland areas of Australia. Tea tree oil, which is used in many types of soaps and shampoos, comes from this plant species.

It is against the law to pick wildflowers in parts of Australia.

55% of a eucalyptus leaf is made up of water.

Australia has more than 700 species of native grass.

About 50 species of mangrove trees exist in Australia.

The stems of a Sturt's desert pea can be up to 6 feet (2 m) long.

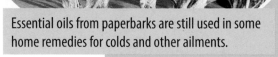

Essential oils from paperbarks are still used in some home remedies for colds and other ailments.

Insects, Reptiles, and Amphibians

Australia is home to a fascinating number and variety of insects, reptiles, and amphibians. Approximately 770 species of reptiles live in Australia. These include snakes, lizards, turtles, and both freshwater and saltwater crocodiles. Within these populations are a large number of dangerous and deadly creatures. In fact, Australia has more species of venomous snakes than anywhere else on Earth. Of the continent's 140 known snake species, 21 are considered deadly. Mosquitoes, honey bees, and bull ants are just a few of the thousands of insect species found in Australia.

The tiger snake can climb trees to prey on birds in their nests.

Tiger Snake

Most Australians can recognize a tiger snake, although not many people will ever see one. Tiger snakes are known to be aggressive and carry toxic venom. These snakes have adapted to some of the harshest environments in the country. The length of a tiger snake can range between 3 feet (91 cm) and about 8 feet (244 cm).

Estuarine Crocodile

The estuarine crocodile is also known as the saltwater crocodile. Estuarine crocodiles are the largest living reptiles on Earth. They are mostly **nocturnal** but have been known to hunt for food during the day. Small crocodiles usually eat insects and crustaceans. A large estuarine crocodile will feed on bigger prey, such as sea turtles.

An estuarine crocodile can grow to as much as 20 feet (6 m) in length.

Bull Ants

Bull ants are a type of insect found throughout Australia. They live in forests and woodlands, and even in urban areas. There are about 90 species of bull ants on the continent. Each has distinct behaviors and life cycles. People should avoid bull ants because they are aggressive and can deliver painful stings. Bull ants range in size from a 0.3 to 1.6 inches (8 to 40 mm).

Young bull ant queens have wings. This allows them to leave the nest and start new colonies.

White-bellied Frog

As its name suggests, the white-bellied frog is best known for its white belly. Its back can be speckled brown or gray, which helps it hide from predators. This frog grows to be about 1 inch (2.5 cm) long. White-bellied frogs are found in a small area on the southwest tip of Australia. They are considered an endangered species.

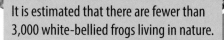

It is estimated that there are fewer than 3,000 white-bellied frogs living in nature.

Just the Facts

The funnel-web spider is the most feared spider in Australia.

Australia has **350** species of mosquitoes.

Of the world's 25 most venomous snakes, 20 live in Australia.

Australia's inland taipan has the most toxic venom of all land snakes. One bite can kill at least 100 humans.

Birds and Mammals

Out of the estimated 750 bird species in Australia, about 350 are not found anywhere else in the world. Australia's birds range from small honeyeaters to the large, flightless emu. The largest **predatory** animal is the dingo, or "wild dog." Other **carnivorous** animals native to Australia include the numbat, Tasmanian devil, and quoll. Marsupials, such as the kangaroo, and egg-laying mammals, such as the platypus, are examples of mammals only found in Australia.

Koalas in the cooler parts of Australia are larger and have thicker fur than those in warmer regions.

Koala

Koalas are very popular Australian mammals. They are found all along the country's temperate eastern coast and in eucalypt forests. Koalas rely on certain types of eucalypts for food. The koala is a marsupial. The young stay in their mother's pouch for about 6 months. A koala is often called a "koala bear," but in fact, it is not a part of the bear family.

Kookaburra

Australia is home to two kookaburra species. The best-known species is the laughing kookaburra. This bird makes a call at dusk and dawn that sounds like someone laughing. The laughing kookaburra can be found in rural areas or city suburbs. Its habitat usually includes plenty of trees. The laughing kookaburra's call is not a laugh but a warning to other birds to stay away.

The laughing kookaburra is a carnivore. It preys on insects, snakes, frogs, and rats.

Emu

Australia's tallest native bird is the emu. It can grow to about 6 feet (2 m) tall. The emu is endemic to Australia. It lives in most regions of the continent, except for the rainforests and very dry areas. Emus are mostly found in savanna woodlands. They roam to find food and water, but will stay in one area if resources are available. Emus eat fruits, seeds, insects, and other small animals.

The emu does not fly, but it can run as quickly as 30 miles (48 km) per hour.

Platypus

The platypus is an egg-laying mammal that lives both on land and in water. It moves smoothly through water using its webbed feet but is slightly awkward when moving on land. This mammal is easily recognized by its bill, which is similar to that of a duck.

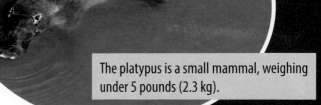

The platypus is a small mammal, weighing under 5 pounds (2.3 kg).

Just the Facts

A koala can eat about 2.2 pounds (1 kg) of eucalyptus leaves per day.

The platypus and echidna are the only egg-laying mammals found on Earth.

An emu can jump 7 feet (2.1 m) straight up into the air.

Australian Aquatic Biomes

Besides its land biomes, Australia also has an abundance of plants and animals living in its waters. Some are found in the marine biome, while others make their home in the freshwater biome. The factor that separates the marine biome from the freshwater biome is the amount of salt content in the water.

Aquatic Ecosystems and Habitats

Aquatic biomes consist of a variety of ecosystems and habitats that support plants and animals. Australia's oceans support about 4,000 of the 22,000 types of fish found on Earth. These oceans also include 30 of the world's 58 seagrass species. The Great Barrier Reef, the largest coral reef in the world, runs along Australia's east coast. Marine life living here vary from the huge, predatory great white shark and whale shark to the simple bluebottle jellyfish.

Marine Biome

Oceans and coral reefs are part of Australia's marine biome. Oceans are extremely large bodies of water that take up most of Earth's surface. Coral reefs are found in the ocean, in areas that have warm, shallow waters.

Plants: Kelp, seaweed, algae, and seagrass are some of the key plants found in the waters around Australia.

About 3% salt content

Animals: Australia's marine biomes are home to green turtles, dugongs, mollusks, sea snakes, several varieties of dolphins, whales, and sharks, and an abundance of fish species.

There are many freshwater lakes in Australia. The Gippsland Lakes lie along the east coast of Australia. Made up of a series of lagoons, lakes, and marshes, they cover an area of about 232 square miles (600 sq. km). The lakes are home to many rare and endangered species, including the Burrunan dolphin. They also serve as breeding sites for many species of fish and birds. Australia's freshwater fish habitats include lakes, swamps, billabongs, streams, and rivers. Freshwater wetlands are an important habitat for fish, plants, and birds. They also support an assortment of plant communities, including trees, reeds and floating or underwater aquatic plants.

The dugong is a marine mammal found in Australia's warm coastal waters. It feeds on underwater grasses found there.

Freshwater Biome

Unlike the marine biome, the freshwater biome has a low salt concentration. Australia's freshwater biomes include ponds, lakes, streams, rivers, and wetlands. Due to Australia's dry conditions, there are only about 150 types of freshwater fish, including the barramundi, living its waters.

Plants: Algae, grasses, bullrush, and water lilies can be found growing in Australia's freshwater biomes.

Less than **1%** salt content

Animals: Freshwater fish, snails, turtles, crocodiles, and platypuses are just some of the animals living in the Australia's lakes, ponds, and rivers.

Australian Aquatic Life

Australia's oceans and coral reefs have a variety of plant and animal life. In its freshwater biomes, plants and animals are well adapted to the low salt content in the water. The main form of plant life in an aquatic biome is algae. Different species of algae have adapted to thrive in either marine or freshwater biomes. Algae take in carbon dioxide from the atmosphere and transform it into oxygen. Most organisms need oxygen to survive.

The whale shark has distinctive body markings that scientists use to identify individuals living in an area.

Whale Shark

The whale shark is the largest fish in the world. It moves slowly through tropical and warm temperate waters off the coast of Australia. Here, the whale shark feeds on small crustaceans, squid, and fish, which it catches by swimming through the water with its mouth open. Whale sharks are huge, but they are not a threat to humans.

Reef Stonefish

Reef stonefish are found throughout tropical and marine waters. They are not easy to spot because they can be **camouflaged** to look like a rock on the sea floor. The reef stonefish usually waits for fish to swim past and then attacks. It does not swim away when bothered by other marine species. It will simply raise its poisonous dorsal fin spines as a warning. Sharks and rays are known to prey on reef stonefish.

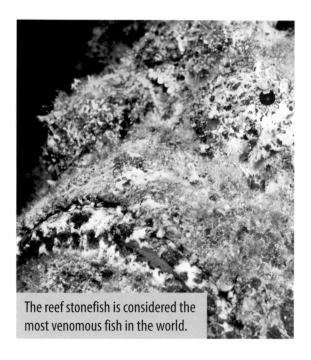
The reef stonefish is considered the most venomous fish in the world.

Box Jellyfish

The box jellyfish is also known as the "sea wasp." This extremely large jellyfish has a box-shaped bell and up to 60 tentacles. These tentacles are nearly 10 feet (3 m) long and full of venom. The stings can stun and kill a fish in minutes. Box jellyfish are found in tropical coastal waters and appear most often in summer.

Each of the box jellyfish's long tentacles can have up to 5,000 stingers.

Green Sea Turtle

The green sea turtle can be found in the coastal waters around Australia. Its name comes from the color of its fat rather than the color of its shell. Strong front flippers help it move through the water. Adults feed on seagrass and algae, but young green turtles are carnivorous. Green turtles can grow to 47 inches (120 cm) in length. All green turtles found in Australia's waters are protected by law.

Green sea turtles can live for more than 80 years.

Just the Facts

Astronauts can see the Great Barrier Reef from space.

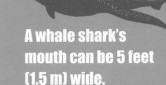

A whale shark's mouth can be 5 feet (1.5 m) wide.

The blue-ringed octopus is one of the most venomous animals in the ocean.

Six species of sea turtle come to the Great Barrier Reef to breed.

The box jellyfish has 24 eyes.

Maintaining Balance

Ecosystems with high biodiversity are usually stronger than those with fewer species. This is because all species in an ecosystem are interconnected and depend on one another for survival. Some species are the food source for others. Some species provide shelter or protection for others. In an ecosystem with less biodiversity, a change in one factor can change the interactions between plants, animals, and their environment. These changes can harm all species in an ecosystem.

Introducing New Species

Biodiversity can be affected when a new species is introduced into an ecosystem. Foreign species often have no natural predators. As a result, the size of the new population will continue to increase.

When Europeans arrived in Australia in the early 1600s, they greatly impacted the country's plant and animal life. Europeans introduced new species into Australia, including foxes, pigs, and rabbits. The introduction of these species affected the balance of the ecosystems. They began crowding, and even killing, Australia's native species. In the past, this change was less of a worry. Today, there is a greater understanding of the ecological problems caused by the introduction of new species.

The red fox was brought to Australia in the late 1800s. Since then, it has become a major threat to many of Australia's native bird and mammal species.

Ecosystem Interactions

All living things in an ecosystem are connected. They are each part of a food chain. A food chain shows the transfer of energy from organism to organism. Plants are producers because they use the Sun's energy to make food. Primary consumers are the herbivores that eat plants. Secondary consumers are carnivores, which eat primary consumers. Decomposers break down dead organisms and put nutrients back into the soil for growing plants.

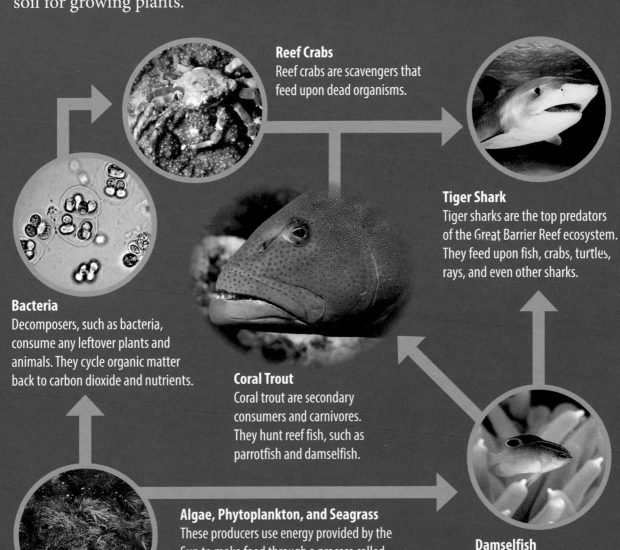

Reef Crabs
Reef crabs are scavengers that feed upon dead organisms.

Tiger Shark
Tiger sharks are the top predators of the Great Barrier Reef ecosystem. They feed upon fish, crabs, turtles, rays, and even other sharks.

Bacteria
Decomposers, such as bacteria, consume any leftover plants and animals. They cycle organic matter back to carbon dioxide and nutrients.

Coral Trout
Coral trout are secondary consumers and carnivores. They hunt reef fish, such as parrotfish and damselfish.

Algae, Phytoplankton, and Seagrass
These producers use energy provided by the Sun to make food through a process called photosynthesis. They also provide food for the many herbivores that live in the ocean.

Damselfish
These primary consumers are herbivores. They feed on the available plant materials.

Diversity for Humans

Australia is home to between 600,000 and 700,000 plant and animal species. These species continue to be an important source of food and shelter. They act as an important resource for people in Australia and all over the world. Australia's natural habitats provide a variety of plants and animals for human consumption. For example, forests and wetlands provide timber and crops that benefit people. The diversity of Australia's ecosystems greatly benefits the Australian people. Certain human actions, however, have had a negative impact upon the country's biodiversity.

The Great Barrier Reef is a popular tourist spot. Millions of people visit each year to experience the biodiversity of this biome.

Human Impact

Since Europeans settled in Australia, more than 50 species of animals and at least 60 species of plants have become **extinct**. New plants and animals were introduced, and land was cleared for urban development and agriculture. These activities have affected Australia's biodiversity. Clearing land has caused soil erosion all over the continent and has destroyed animal habitats. The koala is just one of many animals that have been affected by this activity. As trees were cleared from its habitat, the koala began losing the eucalypt trees it uses for food and shelter. Koala populations declined as a result. Other factors that affect animal and plant populations include pollution, overfishing, and overhunting.

Land that is rich in natural vegetation is often most at risk for clear-cutting.

Conserving Nature

Australians are working hard to **conserve** the country's biodiversity. All over the continent, governments, environmental groups, and individuals have set up programs to **preserve** Australia's ecosystems and habitats. Australia's National Reserve System is playing a key role in these conservation efforts. In 2008, the Natural Reserve System included more than 10,000 parks and reserves covering approximately 560,000 square miles (900,000 sq. km). The government also manages the protection of six national parks, two botanic gardens, and 27 marine protected areas.

These protected areas preserve Australia's biodiversity. Through conservation, it is hoped that Australia's unique plant and animal species, and its beautiful land and marine areas, can also be preserved.

The smallest penguin species, sometimes called the fairy penguin, can be found in Port Campbell National Park, one of the National Reserve System's many parks.

Make an Ecosystem Web

Use this book and research on the internet to create an Australian ecosystem.

1. Find an Australian plant or animal. Think about what habitat it lives in.

2. Find at least three organisms that are found in the same habitat. These organisms could include plants, insects, amphibians, reptiles, birds, and mammals.

3. How do these species interact with each other? Do they provide food or shelter for the organisms?

4. Begin linking these organisms together to show which organisms rely on each other for food or shelter.

5. Once your ecosystem web is complete, think about how removing one organism would affect the other organisms in the web.

Australian Coral Reef Ecosystem

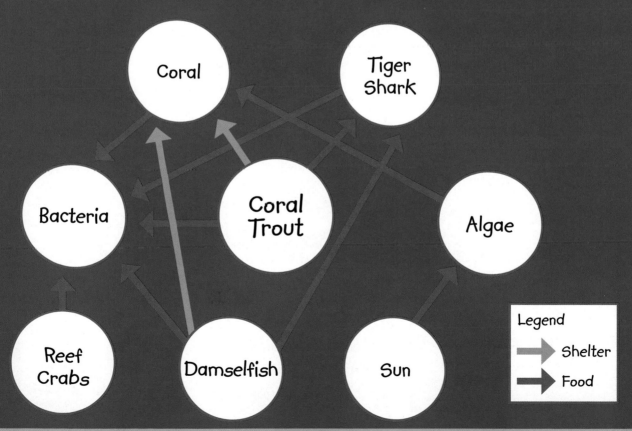

Quiz

1 What are the three main land biomes found in Australia?

Deserts, rainforests, and grassland

2 What is an endemic species?

A plant or animal that is only found in one part of the world

3 Which three oceans border Australia?

Pacific, Indian, and Southern Oceans

6 How many species of eucalypts are there?

About 28,000

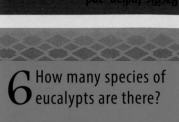

4 How much of Australia is covered with spinifex grasslands?

22 percent

5 How many of Australia's snake species are considered deadly?

21

9 When did Europeans first arrive in Australia?

1600s

7 In what biome is the kangaroo typically found?

Grassland

10 Name one invasive animal species introduced by Europeans.

The red fox

8 Name two ecosystems found within a marine biome.

Ocean and coral reef

Key Words

adapted: changed to suit the environment

biodiversity: the variety of life in a particular habitat or ecosystem

camouflaged: colored or patterned to blend in with the environment

carnivorous: meat-eating animals

conserve: protect something from destruction

coral reefs: underwater structures made up of calcium carbonate and populated by marine organisms

equator: an imaginary horizontal line that marks the center of the Earth

extinct: no longer living on Earth

habitats: environments that are occupied by a particular species of plant, animal, or other kind of organism

nocturnal: primarily active at night

predatory: living by killing and eating other animals

preserve: keep in its original state

rainforests: forests that receive large amounts of rain and that have very tall trees

species: a group of organisms that share similar characteristics

vascular: having channels or tubes for carrying fluids

vertebrates: animals that have backbones

Index

Log on to www.av2books.com

AV[2] by Weigl brings you media enhanced books that support active learning. Go to www.av2books.com, and enter the special code found on page 2 of this book. You will gain access to enriched and enhanced content that supplements and complements this book. Content includes video, audio, weblinks, quizzes, a slide show, and activities.

AV[2] Online Navigation

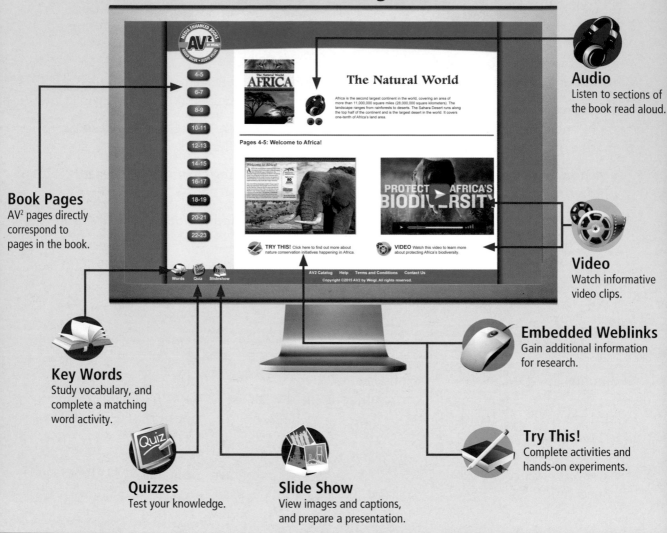

Book Pages
AV[2] pages directly correspond to pages in the book.

Audio
Listen to sections of the book read aloud.

Video
Watch informative video clips.

Embedded Weblinks
Gain additional information for research.

Key Words
Study vocabulary, and complete a matching word activity.

Try This!
Complete activities and hands-on experiments.

Quizzes
Test your knowledge.

Slide Show
View images and captions, and prepare a presentation.

AV[2] was built to bridge the gap between print and digital. We encourage you to tell us what you like and what you want to see in the future.

Sign up to be an AV[2] Ambassador at www.av2books.com/ambassador.

Due to the dynamic nature of the internet, some of the URLs and activities provided as part of AV[2] by Weigl may have changed or ceased to exist. AV[2] by Weigl accepts no responsibility for any such changes. All media enhanced books are regularly monitored to update addresses and sites in a timely manner. Contact AV[2] by Weigl at 1-866-649-3445 or av2books@weigl.com with any questions, comments, or feedback.